THINKING BIBLICALLY ABOUT

CLIMATE CHANGE...

RICHARD BULL

CONNECT: THINKING BIBLICALLY ABOUT CLIMATE CHANGE...

Copyright © Richard Bull 2007
First published 2007
ISBN 978 1 84427 279 2

Scripture Union, 207–209 Queensway, Bletchley, MK2 2EB, England.
Email: info@scriptureunion.org.uk
Website: www.scriptureunion.org.uk

Scripture Union Australia
Locked Bag 2, Central Coast Business Centre, NSW 2252
Website: www.scriptureunion.org.au

Scripture Union USA
PO Box 987, Valley Forge, PA 19482
Website: www.scriptureunion.org

The right of Richard Bull to be identified as author of this work has been asserted by him in
accordance with the Copyright, Designs and Patents Act 1988.

Scripture quotations taken from THE HOLY BIBLE, TODAY'S NEW INTERNATIONAL
VERSION, (TNIV). Copyright © 2004 by International Bible Society. Used by permission of
Hodder & Stoughton Publishers, a division of Hodder Headline Ltd. All rights reserved.
"TNIV" is a registered trademark of International Bible Society.

British Library Cataloguing-in-Publication Data.

A catalogue record of this book is available from the British Library.

Printed and bound in Great Britain by Henry Ling Ltd, Dorchester, England.

Cover and internal design by ie Design of Birmingham, UK
Typesetting by Carsten Lorenz

Scripture Union is an international Christian charity working with churches in more than
130 countries providing resources to bring the good news about Jesus Christ to children, young
people and families – and to encourage them to develop spiritually through the Bible and
prayer.

As well as our network of volunteers, staff and associates who run holidays, church-based
events and school Christian groups, we produce a wide range of publications and support those
who use our resources through training programmes.

CONNECT

John Stott, a former president of Scripture Union, has stressed the need for Christians to 'relate the ancient Word to the modern world.' His vision is for integrated Christians – those who have brought every area of their lives under the lordship of Christ – to penetrate the world. To this end we hope that each booklet in the Connect series will 'do what it says on the tin' – help readers think biblically about the big issues of the day. And, having begun to think biblically about those issues, we pray that readers will feel able to thoughtfully penetrate the world, making a biblical perspective part of their everyday conversations about those issues and part of their own everyday living.

Nigel Hopper
Matt Campbell
Series Editors

CONTENTS

INTRODUCTION

It's 17 January 2007. It's 5 minutes to midnight. And the 'Doomsday Clock' is ticking. It's not a real clock – just a conceptual one – though a real representation is kept on the wall in the Chicago offices of The Bulletin of the Atomic Scientists (BAS). It was this magazine that devised the clock in 1947, originally setting it to 7 minutes to midnight to symbolise the proximity of global nuclear annihilation after America dropped its A-bombs on Japan. Since then the minute hand has been moved backwards or forwards 18 times from the 'Doomsday' midnight hour in response to world events. The most recent change, on 17 January, saw the clock moved forwards 2 minutes, to the time of 5 minutes to midnight. But it wasn't an escalation of nuclear activity that prompted the move. It was, for the first time ever, climate change. Commenting on the decision to put the 'Doomsday Clock' forwards, Sir Martin Rees, the English Astronomer Royal, said 'Humankind's collective impacts on the biosphere, climate and oceans are unprecedented. These environmentally driven threats – "threats without enemies" – should loom as large in the political perspective as did the east/west political divide during the Cold War era.'

But how large should the issue of climate change loom in a Christian perspective?

But how large should the issue of climate change loom in a Christian perspective? Well, that really depends on how large you think it looms, if at all, in a biblical perspective. This booklet won't give you the answer to what constitutes a Christian response to climate change, but it will challenge you to think about how biblical teaching might be used to form such a response. There are no easy answers, but that shouldn't stop us from wrestling with the issues.

In addition to the biblical material we're obviously

also going to have to engage with a fair amount of information about climate change. Now you don't need to know much about climate change yourself to know that there are huge differences of opinion about it among those who do, or who claim to. On the one hand there are those who are convinced the entire planet will be under water within 50 years, and on the other there are those who can't understand what all the fuss is about, insisting that climate change always has and always will be part of the natural order of things. Both camps insist, of course, that their stance is justified by the facts. But if you've got a particular axe to grind you might be tempted to highlight the facts that help you do that and bury the ones that don't. All of which leaves your average author of a booklet on thinking biblically about climate change wondering just where you go to get the real facts, free from any hidden or unhidden agendas. Fortunately, a friend of mine (who, in case you wanted to know, is a lecturer in Geography and Environmental Science) directed me to the Intergovernmental Panel on Climate Change (IPCC). They, he assured me (and he should know), provide genuinely well-researched material and a more balanced perspective on the issue. So when it comes to the facts about climate change included in this booklet I've drawn primarily from the research of the IPCC rather than from business or 'green' groups.

I should say that in a little booklet like this we're inevitably only going to be able to scratch the surface of some complicated environmental, social and theological issues. But this is a conversation-starter, not a conversation-stopper. I hope you'll want to continue the conversation beyond these pages, so I've included references throughout and made suggestions for further reading at the end.

So, where should we begin our biblical thinking about climate change? Well, the very beginning seems like a very good place to start, so let's turn first to creation.

1 CREATION AND CLIMATE CHANGE

With a global debate about climate change and its implications raging all around us it's easy to overlook the fact that the temperature of planet earth has always been subject to change. The average global temperature is currently in the region of 15 °C. Evidence suggests that, in the past, this average may have been as high as 27 °C and as low as 7 °C. The first chapter of Genesis describes how, in the beginning, God created the heavens and the earth. It concludes with the words, 'God saw all that he had made, and it was very good. And there was evening, and there was morning – the sixth day' (Genesis 1:31). Are we to assume, therefore, that climate change is actually built-in to the earth by design and part and parcel of that which God declared 'very good'? Or should we trace the introduction of climate change on the earth only as far back as the fall, regarding it as a consequence of God's curse on the ground (Genesis 3:17)?

Are we to assume, therefore, that climate change is actually built-in to the earth by design and part and parcel of that which God declared 'very good'?

We can answer this question whichever way we like, but deciding when natural climate change became a feature of planet earth doesn't address the issue of why the climate is changing now, warming up with apparently unnatural speed.

Most people have heard of the greenhouse effect – they were talking about this when I was at school (along with things like acid rain) and I'm now 34! The greenhouse effect refers to the role played by naturally occurring gases that effectively trap energy from the sun in the earth's atmosphere. Without them the planet would be too cold to sustain life as we know it. Greenhouse gases include carbon dioxide, methane and nitrous oxide. Their concentration in the atmosphere is increasing – the concentration of carbon dioxide has risen by more than 30 per cent since 1800. It follows that more of the sun's energy will be trapped in the earth's atmosphere, causing a rise in the earth's temperature. Evidence suggests that this is exactly what's happening.

The IPCC presented its latest set of research findings in February 2007. Their report, 'Climate Change 2007: The Physical Science Basis', concluded, among other things, that 'the annual carbon dioxide concentration growth-rate was larger during the last ten years (1995–2005 average: 1.9 ppm [parts per million] per year) than it has been since the beginning of continuous direct atmospheric measurements (1960–2005 average: 1.4 ppm per year)'. Correspondingly, the report projects a rise in globally averaged surface temperature of between 1.8 °C and 4 °C by the end of the century, and a rise in sea levels of between 28 cm and 43 cm. The report also projects an increase in heatwaves and in the intensity of tropical storms.

The possible long-term effects of global warming were recently outlined in a review undertaken for the UK government by former chief economist to the World Bank, Sir Nicholas Stern. His much publicised report included the findings that rising sea levels could displace up to 200 million people, that the risk of flooding will be greatly increased by melting glaciers, and that up to 40 per cent of wildlife species could face extinction.

So, do we have any idea what's brought about this unnatural global warming with its potentially catastrophic consequences? The IPCC certainly think they do. In December 2005 their chairman, Dr Rajendra Pachauri, said, 'The earth's climate system has demonstrably changed on both global and regional scales since the pre-industrial era, and there is new and stronger evidence that most of the warming observed over the last

50 years is attributable to human activities.' One obvious example of such evidence is the knowledge that the activities of modern industry and agriculture, not least the burning of fossil fuels, are known to release greenhouse gases into the atmosphere, thereby increasing their concentration.

Attributing the majority of current global warming to human activity raises the question of our relationship with, and responsibility for, planet earth. And, for a biblical perspective, that takes us back to the opening chapters of Genesis.

According to the first chapter of Genesis, human beings are part of the created order. They share with the whole of creation the fact of being brought into existence by God. However, unlike the rest of creation, human beings are said to be made in God's image (Genesis 1:27) and created '…that they may rule over the fish in the sea and the birds in the sky, over the livestock and all the wild animals, and over all the creatures that move along the ground' (Genesis 1:26). It comes as no surprise, therefore, when God blesses the first man and woman and says to them, 'Be fruitful and increase in number; fill the earth and subdue it. Rule over the fish in the sea and the birds in the sky and over every living creature that moves on the ground' (Genesis 1:28).

'Rule' over the living creatures, 'subdue' the earth… how are we to understand these commands? Can we take them to mean that God expects us to use the earth and its resources for our benefit, no matter what the environmental impact? Do they allow us to write-off climate change as an unfortunate side effect of our subduing the earth through our activity?

'Rule' over the living creatures, 'subdue' the earth… how are we to understand these commands? Can we take them to mean that God expects us to use the earth and its resources for our benefit, no matter what the environmental impact? Do they allow us to write-off climate change as an unfortunate side effect of our subduing the earth through our activity?

Certainly, as James Jones, the Bishop of Liverpool, has noted in his book, *Jesus and the Earth* (SPCK, 2003), Christians have long been accused by the 'green' movement of using these creation commands to justify what the 'greens' regard as an irresponsible and disinterested attitude towards environmental issues. But how else might these commands be understood?

Bishop Jones suggests that the commands in Genesis 1:28 need to be qualified by the words of Genesis 2:15: 'The Lord God took the man and put him in the Garden of Eden to work it and take care of it.' The Hebrew word translated 'take care' has its root in the idea of service. So, should we, with Bishop Jones, see ourselves as 'servant rulers' of the earth? If so, what does that mean in practical terms? Does it mean necessarily being at the forefront of moves to restrict and reverse climate change?

Interestingly, these hotly debated commands are actually repeated in Genesis 9. The context there is God's covenant with Noah after the flood. Or is it? You see, Bible translations like TNIV take the liberty of inserting the section heading 'God's covenant with Noah' at the start of Genesis 9. But, as Peter Harris of the Christian conservation charity, A Rocha, has observed, this skews our reading of the passage. It focuses our attention on Noah as the covenant partner when what the text actually says is that God made his covenant with Noah, his descendants '…and with every living creature that was with you – the birds, the livestock and all the wild animals, all those that came out of the ark with you – every living creature on earth' (Genesis 9:10). And the rainbow, God says, is set in the clouds as a sign of the covenant between him and '…the earth' (Genesis 9:13).

Has God, in this covenant, absolved us of all responsibility for guarding the earth against environmental disaster? Or should the knowledge that God has made his covenant with the earth, as well as with his people, heighten our concern for, and commitment to, the environment?

Should the fact that God has made a covenant with the earth influence our treatment of it? God's promise was, of course, that never again would the earth be destroyed by a flood (Genesis 9:11,15). So does that make anxiety about rising sea levels caused by global warming unnecessary? Has God, in this covenant, absolved us of all responsibility for guarding the earth against environmental disaster? Or should the knowledge that God has made his covenant with the earth, as well as with his people, heighten our concern for, and commitment to, the environment? It might help to take a look at how God's covenant people in the Bible understood their relationship to, and responsibility for, the environment.

2 COVENANT PEOPLE AND CLIMATE CHANGE

It won't surprise you to hear that climate change isn't actually mentioned anywhere in the Old Testament! It wasn't an issue for God's people back then, not least because they had no way of measuring climate change. Nevertheless, we do know quite a bit about their attitude to the environment from looking at their temple worship resource book – the Psalms. 'The earth is the LORD's, and everything in it, the world, and all who live in it; for he founded it on the seas and established it on the waters', so proclaims Psalm 24:1,2. Whatever God's people made of the Genesis command to 'subdue' the earth, they evidently didn't take it to mean that God had transferred ownership of the earth to them. Should we assume, therefore, that they saw themselves only as caretakers of the earth? They certainly seem to have appreciated the beauty and majesty of the earth entrusted to them, regarding it as an inspiration to praise: 'When I consider your heavens, the work of your fingers, the moon and the stars, which you have set in place, what are mere mortals that you are mindful of them, human beings that you care for them?' (Psalm 8:3). Likewise, Psalm 19:1 expresses a similar theme: 'The heavens declare the glory of God; the skies proclaim the work of his hands.' Does it follow that the current estimated loss of 40 species every day (www.rainforestinfo.org.au)

due to the deforestation of an area the size of Wales each year in the Amazon rainforest (itself a cause of climate change) is a loss of God-given incentives to praise him? In light of the psalmist's words, is Archbishop Daniel of Moldova right to say that 'extinction is a loss of our knowledge of God – we're erasing his fingerprints' (quoted by Ruth Valerio in 'Globalisation and the Environment', *One World or Many – The impact of Globalisation on Mission*, edited by Richard Tiplady, Paternoster Press, 2003), or is the extinction of some species the regrettable but inevitable outcome of human beings obeying the creation command to 'Be fruitful and increase in number' (Genesis 1:28)?

… is the extinction of some species the regrettable but inevitable outcome of human beings obeying the creation command to 'Be fruitful and increase in number' (Genesis 1:28)?

Psalm 96 demands that we consider a further possibility; that our impact on climate and the environment affects not only our ability to praise God but also that of creation itself:

Let the heavens rejoice, let the earth be glad;
let the sea resound, and all that is in it.
Let the fields be jubilant, and everything in them;
let all the trees of the forest sing for joy.
Let all creation rejoice before the Lord, for he comes,
he comes to judge the earth.

(Psalm 96:11–13)

How will the rainforest sing for joy if there are no trees left there to give it voice?

The mention of God coming to judge the earth in Psalm 96 reminds us of a key facet of God's character as portrayed in the Bible. As Creator and Lord of all the earth, God alone is judge of all the earth. So, when we read of God in Psalm 89:9 that, 'You rule over the surging sea; when its waves mount up, you still them', should we conclude that rising sea levels and events like the tsunami of 2004 are signs that God in his judgement is choosing not to still the surging seas? After all, outside the Psalms the prophets speak of God's judgement in terms that could be taken as implying an environmental impact. 'See, the Lord is go-

Could these prophecies, and others like them, now be being fulfilled through the effects of climate change, or is such an understanding a misunderstanding and misuse of the Bible?

ing to lay waste the earth and devastate it', says Isaiah 24:1. Similarly, Jeremiah 25:32 has God describing his wrath, saying 'Look! Disaster is spreading from nation to nation; a mighty storm is rising from the ends of the earth.' Could these prophecies, and others like them, now be being fulfilled through the effects of climate change, or is such an understanding a misunderstanding and misuse of the Bible?

So it looks like God's covenant people regarded the earth as belonging to God, as both inspiring and being capable of offering praise and worship to God, and as being subject to judgement by God. We don't know too much about the extent to which this view of the earth shaped an environmentally-friendly people of God, but we do know it didn't stop them undertaking huge building projects that couldn't fail to have an impact on the environment. Take the building of the temple as recorded in 1 Kings 6 and 2 Chronicles 2–4. The brief was a structure that would be 'large and magnificent' (2 Chronicles 2:9). And, as you'll see if you read those chapters, it certainly was! But think about the environmental impact. Vast numbers of trees were cut down – cedar, juniper and algum, sourced not locally (ie from Israel) but from Lebanon (2 Chronicles 2:8), and almost certainly not from sustainably managed forests. Can we therefore see this project as a very early contributor to climate change? If so, can we say that climate change is acceptable when brought about by activities that are the means to the end of glorifying God? If we can then, presumably, we can also use this biblical account to justify the conscripting of forced labour to realise our grand and God-glorifying dreams in line with Solomon's actions (1 Kings 5:13,14).

… can we say that climate change is acceptable when brought about by activities that are the means to the end of glorifying God?

But looked at from another perspective, would a recycled, energy-efficient temple have been quite so glorifying to God? This isn't just a theoretical question. Many churches will find themselves prayerfully considering a building project at some point in their life. They want to give glory to God, but do they do that by building a 'large and magnificent' structure or by building something simple that is economical and energy-efficient to produce and maintain?

Talking of church, we have so far in our discussion on covenant people and climate change been focused on what in biblical terms is the old covenant. At the Last Supper, Jesus spoke of his impending death as establishing and sealing a new covenant to provide for the forgiveness of sins (see Luke 22:20, Matthew 26:28 and Jeremiah 31:33,34). So, does the new covenant have environmental implications? What did the first New Testament Christians think?

To be honest, there's not much to go on. There are, however, a couple of significant passages in Paul's letters. First, there's Colossians 1:15–20. Here we learn that not only did Christ create all things, but also that they were created for him (v 16). In a sense this simply confirms the psalmist's assertion that the earth is the Lord's. But put this way, doesn't it have the added dimension of implying that we might, through the effects of climate change, actually be stealing from Christ that which was made for him?

Second, there's Romans 8:19–21, where Paul says, 'The creation waits in eager expectation for the children of God to be revealed. For the creation was subjected to frustration, not by its own choice, but by the will of the one who subjected it, in the hope that the creation itself will be liberated from its bondage to decay and brought into the freedom and glory of the children of God.' If the language of subjection recalls the curse on the earth resulting from the fall in Genesis 3:17, doesn't the language of liberation recall God's covenant commitment to the earth in Genesis 9:13? And doesn't it anticipate John's vision, recorded in Revelation 21:1, of a new heaven and a new earth?

Is it possible that efforts to reduce and reverse climate change are misguided and constitute the storing up of treasure on earth rather than in heaven? Or should the promise of a new earth spur us to a new level of creation care?

It has been said to me that if we're going to receive a new heaven and a new earth then we're wasting our time trying to preserve this earth. Is it possible that efforts to reduce and reverse climate change are misguided and constitute the storing up of treasure on earth rather than in heaven? Or should the promise of a new earth spur us to a new level of creation care? Bishop Tom Wright thinks so. He suggests that the resurrection of Jesus is a model for what God will do for the earth. Just as Christ was raised with a renewed rather than a replacement body so, thinks Wright, creation will be renewed rather than replaced. The new earth of Revelation 21 will be, in Wright's words, 'A world which is creation renewed, where God has done for the whole cosmos at the last what he did for Jesus at Easter. In other words, a re-embodiment, a vibrant life which does not decay or corrupt' (*Creation and New Creation in the New Testament*, available from www. regentaudio.com).

Does how we respond or fail to respond to climate change now have eternal consequences for the earth?

Jesus' resurrected body still bore the marks of his crucifixion. So, if Wright is correct and if we're not careful, could even the new earth bear the marks of climate change? Does how we respond or fail to respond to climate change now have eternal consequences for the earth?

Having thought about covenant people and climate change in both the Old and New Testaments the question – and it's a crucial one for Christians – that still remains is what, if anything, would Jesus do about climate change?

3 CHRIST AND CLIMATE CHANGE

Once again, you won't be surprised to hear that Jesus says nothing in the New Testament about climate change. Bishop James Jones admits that prior to writing his book, *Jesus and the Earth*, he thought that Jesus said precious little about the earth. Having researched his book though, Jones was able to include a comprehensive section on Jesus' sayings about the earth – it's well worth a look if you want your thinking about climate change, and other environmental issues, to be further informed by the Bible. For Jones, one of Christ's key sayings about the earth is Matthew 5:34,35, where Jesus says, 'But I tell you, do not swear an oath at all: either by heaven, for it is God's throne; or by the earth, for it is his footstool…' 'Herein …' argues Jones, '… lies the sacredness of the earth and the theological truth upon which Christians form an ethic about the earth. The reason we respect and cherish the earth is precisely because it is God's footstool, his resting place.' Is he right? If he is, we can presumably cite this verse as a basis for Christian concern about, and action on, climate change. But might Jesus' words not simply be a picture of the greatness of God?

So, does the knowledge that Jesus is Lord of creation have any bearing on our thinking about climate change?

Much of the content of the Gospels is designed to present Jesus as the Son of God. This includes various 'nature miracles' (the stilling of the storm, walking on water etc) that reveal Jesus as Lord of all creation in a way that the Jews of his day would have associated with God himself. So, does the knowledge that Jesus is Lord of creation have any bearing on our thinking about climate change? We could take the view that we should not spoil that which Christ is Lord over. The trouble is that whilst there's plenty of biblical evidence of Christ's concern for the people of his creation, there doesn't appear to be much evidence of his concern for the environment of his creation. In fact, there's possibly more evidence to the contrary. For example, he apparently places a much greater value on human life than he does on that of a sparrow (Matthew 10:29–31). He refers seemingly casually to the burning of flowers and grass (Matthew 6:30). And then there's his cursing of the fig tree (Mark 11:12–26). This was apparently for no other reason than that he found no figs on the tree to satisfy his hunger. But then it wasn't the season for figs. Sure, the withering of the tree again shows Jesus to be Lord of creation, but does it also show him to be up for a bit of environmental destruction in order to make a theological point? Perhaps the rules are different when you're the Lord of creation? Does one fig tree matter anyway? Alternatively, is this just a red herring in regard to Christ and climate change?

Sure, the withering of the tree again shows Jesus to be Lord of creation, but does it also show him to be up for a bit of environmental destruction in order to make a theological point?

Interestingly, although Jesus makes no specific reference to climate change, he does anticipate what we might term environmental changes. In Matthew 24, describing signs of the 'end times', he says to his disciples 'There will be famines and earthquakes in various places. All these are the beginning of birth-pains' (vs 7,8). And he goes on to say, 'immediately after the distress of those days "the sun will be darkened, and the moon will not give its light; the stars will fall from the sky, and the heavenly bodies will be shaken"' (v 29). Could those famines and the darkening of the sun result from climate change? If so, should we actually positively welcome climate change as warming us up for the return of Christ?

All of this should not blind us to the fact that the Gospel evidence of Christ's concern for the people of his creation also has implications for our thinking about climate change. Take, for example, Jesus' statement that there are no greater commandments than 'Love the Lord your God with all your heart and with all your soul and with all your mind and with all your strength' and 'Love your neighbour as yourself' (Mark 12:30,31). Apart from enjoying milder winters and warmer summers, many readers of this booklet might feel somewhat detached from the alleged consequences of climate change. As a result, it's all too easy to regard it as someone else's problem. But doesn't the command to love our neighbour as ourselves make it our problem as well?

It is generally agreed that it is some of the world's poorest countries, who have contributed least to the problem of climate change, who will suffer its effects the most. Michael Northcott notes, for example, that in Bangladesh 10 per cent of the population live on land that would be flooded regularly if sea levels rose by just 50 cm (The Environment and Christian Ethics, CUP, 1996). Climate change is already affecting people across Africa and there is a growing consensus that future global warming will simply compound the problems and wipe out efforts to tackle poverty there unless urgent action is taken ('Up in Smoke' by Andrew Simms of the New Economics Foundation). If we lived in Bangladesh or Africa, wouldn't we want Christians in the West to love us as they love themselves in regard to climate change and its effects? Wouldn't we want them to display the same concern for the poor so characteristic of Jesus', who launched his ministry manifesto with the words (from Isaiah 61:1), 'The Spirit of the Lord is on me, because he has anointed me to proclaim good news to the poor' (Luke 4:18)?

If we lived in Bangladesh or Africa, wouldn't we want Christians in the West to love us as they love themselves in regard to climate change and its effects?

Jesus, according to the Gospel writers, didn't just proclaim the good news, he was the good news, just as he was 'the way and the truth and the life' (John 14:6). This is why he was able to send out the twelve with the message, 'The kingdom of heaven has come near' (Matthew 10:7). So, having considered some of the things Jesus said, is there anything in what he did – in how he lived – that can help us in our thinking about what we should do and how we should live in response to climate change?

4 CHRIST, CHRISTIANS AND CLIMATE CHANGE

Jesus' material circumstances owe to his knowledge of his particular mission and the time in which he had to complete it?

Put simply, Jesus lived simply. Responding to a teach er of the law who came to him and said 'Teacher, I wi follow you wherever you go', Jesus replied, 'Foxes have holes and birds have nests, but the Son of Man has nowhere to lay his head' (Matthew 8:19,20). Jesus it seems, had no home of his own. It follows that he had few, if any, possessions. So, when he asks the rich young man (Mark 10:21) and his disciples to sell all their possessions (Luke 12:33), isn't he asking no mor than that they live like him? Similarly, can't many of Jesus' teachings on wealth and possessions be under-stood as inviting his hearers to live as he lived? For example, though poor in worldly terms, Jesus was ric towards God (Luke 12:21). And didn't he evidently serve God rather than money (Matthew 6:24)? But then again, how much did Jesus' material circumstan es owe to his knowledge of his particular mission and the time in which he had to complete it?

One of the major contributing factors to climate change is the phenomenal level of demand that our contemporary lifestyles place on the earth's resources Our demands on the natural world have tripled since 1961 (www.wwf.org.uk). It's all too easy to live under the assumption that our planet is a bottomless pit, a deep well of resources that will never run out. The reality is that the earth's renewable resources – like water, timber or fish – are rapidly being exhausted (figures from www.countdown2010.net suggest that the over-capacity of the European fishing fleet has left 80 per cent of marine fish stocks facing collapse) and our use and disposal of non-renewable resources is radically altering our environment. 'Counting Consumption', a recent report by the World Wide Fund for Nature (WWF), warned that the world's ecosystems are being degraded at an unprecedented rate, and that 'it would require three planets to support the world's consumption if everyone used as many of the earth's available resources as the average UK resident'.

All this consumption generates over 100 million tonnes of waste each year, of which household waste is a significant proportion (www.defra.gov.uk). Despite a notable increase in recycling, almost 70 per cent of this waste is disposed of in landfill sites – literally buried in a great big hole. This is a big problem for two reasons. First, if we carry on like this we're eventually going to run out of space in which to dig the holes to bury our rubbish. Second, and more ominously, rubbish buried in landfill sites generates methane – a greenhouse gas 21 times more potent than carbon dioxide (www.defra.gov.uk).

You've probably heard of 'carbon footprints'. A 'carbon footprint' is 'a measure of the impact human activities have on the environment in terms of the amount of greenhouse gases produced, measured in units of carbon dioxide' (www.carbonfootprint.com). The larger a person's (or a country's) 'carbon footprint', the more damaging is their impact on climate change and the environment. All sorts of everyday activities contribute to our carbon footprint, but in general terms four areas of our lives generate four fifths of our overall impact on the environment: how we run our homes, the food we eat, how we travel at home and how we travel on holiday. In the UK, transport accounts for 20 per cent of the average person's carbon footprint, and a further 25 per cent comes from the food we eat – through the way it's produced, packaged and delivered to our shops or homes (WWF). Can anyone dispute the fact that the average UK resident is leaving behind a much larger 'carbon footprint' than Jesus did through his simple lifestyle when he was on earth?

Should our purchasing (ie consumption) habits as Christians be different from those of non-Christians?

Assuming there's no argument, what, if anything, should our response be? Should our purchasing (ie consumption) habits as Christians be different from those of non-Christians? Should we, for example, resist updating our wardrobes with the latest fashions until the clothes and shoes we already own have worn out? Should we be content with our CD players, so long as they work, rather than make them redundant with the purchase of an iPod? How should we approach the ownership of a digital television given the waste mountain of old sets that will inevitably rise up when the analogue signal is switched off and everyone is faced with 'going digital'? Should the knowledge that a car (typically doing 40 miles to the gallon) saves in one year the energy equivalent to 400 years' worth of glass recycling cause us to regard the driving of 'sports utility vehicles' (which typically do only 20 miles to the gallon) as irresponsible? (Figures from 'Towards Greener Households' by The Industry Council for Packaging and the Environment, www.incpen. org.) And, given that the airline industry is predicted to become one of the largest single sources of carbon emissions, should Christians now commit to holidaying at home rather than abroad? What about our food – should we eat only locally-sourced produce? And should that produce, as far as possible, be fresh and free of packaging?

… do we, in our day and age, need to start seeing such inconveniences and the placing of limits on our consumption as part of the cost of our discipleship?

All of this, of course, implies drastic changes to our everyday outlook and lifestyles. To act on any one of the above suggestions would no doubt greatly inconvenience us. But do we, in our day and age, need to start seeing such inconveniences and the placing of limits on our consumption as part of the cost of our discipleship? To this end, do we need to make a fresh commitment to tithing, a principle that effectively serves, among other things, to limit our consumption? True, it's an Old Testament principle (see Leviticus 27:30), but don't Paul's words in 1 Corinthians 16:2 sound very much like a New Testament application of the same principle to the Christian community?

In thinking about the implications of Jesus' lifestyle for Christian living it's important to remember that he himself wasn't averse to occasional outbursts of extravagance. Quite apart from it being an amazing symbol of his generosity and a sign of the coming of the kingdom of God, wasn't Jesus' turning of water into wine at the wedding in Cana (John 2:1–10) an act of extravagance that quite possibly resulted in over-consumption? And when Jesus was anointed with a jar of expensive perfume by a woman at Bethany (Mark 14:3–9) some of those present expressed indignation at the apparent waste (vs 4,5), but Jesus described the extravagant act as 'a beautiful thing' (v 6). And just how do you suppose Jesus gained a reputation as a 'glutton and a drunkard' (Luke 7:34)?

The Gospels do read, though, as if these occasional outbursts of extravagance were just that – occasional. Extravagance seems to have been the exception for Jesus, and the simplicity of life advocated by the Old Testament wisdom books (see, for example, Proverbs 19:1; 23:4,5; 30:7,8) the norm. But before we go out and sell all our possessions, including, presumably, this booklet, it's also important to recognise that Jesus himself benefited from the generosity of those who had homes and possessions and were willing to share them with him. In Luke 8, for example, we read that various women travelled about with Jesus and his disciples and helped to support them 'out of their own means' (v 3). Needs were met, it seems, within the community of Jesus' followers. Similarly, as PH Davids has noted, the rich young man was told not only to sell all his possessions and give to the poor, but also to follow Jesus (Mark 10:21). 'In other words', says Davids, 'the call to radical generosity is at one level an individual decision, but its context is that of a call to a community' ('Rich and Poor' in *Dictionary of Jesus and the Gospels*, IVP, 1992). That is to say, although the rich young man would become financially dependent, he would join the community of disciples who, as we see later in Acts 2:44,45, 'had everything in common' and 'sold property and possessions to give to anyone who had need'. What are the practical implications of this for our churches?

As a church community at Trent Vineyard in Nottingham we've begun asking questions about our environmental impact, both in terms of the building and the people. So we've conducted an environmental audit of the building, looking at energy and water use, recycling etc. We've switched over to energy efficient bulbs, implemented recycling and we're currently looking at trying to encourage car sharing. We've established a regular 'World Service' event, at which we try to raise congregational awareness on global and environmental issues. (Visit www.trentvineyard.org.uk for more information.)

… could churches perhaps also consider encouraging people who live in close proximity to share household appliances such as washing machines, vacuum cleaners and lawn mowers? Should they, if necessary, be encouraging people to live in closer proximity so that having 'everything in common' is a more realistic possibility? Or would this be a misguided attempt to recreate a first-century lifestyle in the twenty-first century?

In the United States, Boise Vineyard now run church allotments that combine creation care with the provision of fresh produce to feed the hungry (see Tri Robinson, *Saving God's Green Earth*, Ampelon, 2006).

Beyond these examples, could churches perhaps also consider encouraging people who live in close proximity to share household appliances such as washing machines, vacuum cleaners and lawn mowers? Should they, if necessary, be encouraging people to live in closer proximity so that having 'everything in common' is a more realistic possibility? Or would this be a misguided attempt to recreate a first-century lifestyle in the twenty-first century?

CLIMATE CHANGE AND DISCIPLESHIP

The nature of the Connect series means that we've raised many more questions in regard to thinking biblically about climate change than we've found answers. I can't tell, of course, what your initial response has been to those questions as you've made your way through this booklet, nor what it will be as you continue to wrestle with those questions beyond this booklet. I can tell you, though, that I feel challenged as a result of writing this booklet. I live with my wife and two young children in Nottingham. We're a two-minute walk from a Co-op food store that's open from 7 am until 10 pm Monday to Saturday and from 10 am until 4 pm on Sundays. We take it for granted that we'll be able to get those things we need in a hurry from its shelves, just as we take it for granted that our local supermarket will stock everything on our weekly shopping list. We're a ten-minute bus ride from the city centre, where we can shop, eat, or drink coffee the whole year round in air-conditioned comfort. Our house is centrally heated and our car climate controlled. I'm beginning to wonder whether my lifestyle, characterised as it is by convenience, comfort and climate control, isn't actually clouding my sense of being an integral part of God's complete creation – of being inter-connected with the environment. And I wonder if this loss of a sense of inter-connectedness with the environment might make me and others like me less able to appreciate the significance of the issue of climate change. I wonder if we need to get out more.

Doesn't Romans 1:20 suggest that God's power and his character are on display in nature? This being so, shouldn't we be attaching more importance to spending time outside, enjoying the beauty of creation?

Doesn't Romans 1:20 suggest that God's power and his character are on display in nature? This being so, shouldn't we be attaching more importance to spending time outside, enjoying the beauty of creation? It's dawned on me in writing this booklet that to spend time in a forest, or on a beach, or up on a mountain is actually to spend time touching the handiwork of God that somehow displays his character. If we can spend more time doing this then might not the issue of climate change and its potential impact take on a whole new significance for us?

We've seen, of course, that climate change isn't only about rising temperatures and sea levels – that's just the tip of the melting iceberg. It's also about the depletion of natural resources and the corresponding need for sustainable consumption. So even if current changes in temperature and sea levels are nothing more than a blip, as some people (and you yourself) might believe, there remain wider environmental issues that present profound challenges to us and our planet. Don't these challenges require us as Christians to continue to think biblically about how those issues should be addressed? And it's a fact that it really is us who need to address these issues. It's safe to assume that most people reading this will, like me, be inhabitants of the developed, Western world. Together we make up only 20 per cent of the world's population, but together we consume 80 per cent of the world's resources. Therefore if, as John Stott (quoting the Church of England's Board for Social Responsibility in his book *Issues Facing Christians Today*, Zondervan, 2006) has written, 'despoiling the earth is a blasphemy', then isn't it we who are taking the Lord's name (and his earth) in vain?

This booklet will be published in 2007 – the bicentenary year of the abolition of slavery in the British Empire. Not so long ago Brian McLaren, a leading figure in the emerging church scene, challenged an audience he was speaking to by comparing the issue of our care for the environment to that of slavery. He invited

In this bicentenary year much is (quite rightly) being made of William Wilberforce, the Christian social reformer whose tireless efforts brought about the abolition of slavery. Should we as Christians, following the example of Wilberforce, be leading the way in responding to the challenges of climate change?

us to consider whether future generations of Christians will look back on us and be appalled that we refused to change our lifestyles even when we knew the damage we were doing to the environment, just as we now look back in history and are appalled that Christians once participated in slavery. What do you think? In this bicentenary year much is (quite rightly) being made of William Wilberforce, the Christian social reformer whose tireless efforts brought about the abolition of slavery. Should we as Christians, following the example of Wilberforce, be leading the way in responding to the challenges of climate change?

FURTHER READING

BOOKS

Harris, P, *Is Caring for Creation a Christian Imperative?*, Regent Audio Bookstore, 2003 (www.regentaudio.com).
Hart, J, *What are they saying about Environmental Theology?*, Paulist Press, 2004.
Mercer, N, 'Postmodernity and Rationality', *Mission and Meaning*, ed A Billington, T Lane and M Turner, Paternoster, 1995.
Peterson, EH, *Christ Plays in Ten Thousand Places*, Hodder & Stoughton, 2005.
Prance, G, *The Earth Under Threat: A Christian Perspective*, Wild Goose Publications, 1996.
Valerio, R, *L is for Lifestyle*, IVP, 2004.

WEBSITES

CLIMATE CHANGE
www.ipcc.ch (The Intergovernmental Panel on Climate Change)
www.climatechallenge.gov.uk
www.stopclimatechaos.org (Stop Climate Chaos is a coalition of leading development organisations, faith communities and charities committed to campaigning against climate change.)

THE NATURAL WORLD
www.arocha.org (A Rocha is a leading, innovative Christian nature conservation organisation.)
www.greenfacts.org
www.countdown2010.net
www.wwf.org.uk

SUSTAINABLE CONSUMPTION AND PRODUCTION
www.wwf.org.uk/oneplanetliving ('One Planet Living' is the latest campaign by WWF.)
www.generous.org.uk

WASTE AND RECYCLING
www.defra.gov.uk/environment/waste
www.wrap.org.uk/retail
www.incpen.org
www.recyclenow.com
www.freecycle.org

CHURCH ACTION

www.savinggodsgreenearth.com
www.letstendthegarden.org
www.ecocongregation.org (Eco-Congregation is an ecumenical programme helping churches make the link between environmental issues and Christian faith, and respond in practical action in the church, in the lives of individuals, and in the local and global community.)